C000229421

Soho Theatre Compa

Flush

by David Dipper

First performed at Soho Theatre on 20 April 2004

Soho Theatre is supported by

Bloomberg **getty**images TBWA\GGT

Performances in the Lorenz Auditorium

Registered Charity No: 267234

Soho Theatre Company productions are supported by the Garfield Weston Foundation. The Writers' Attachment programme is supported by The Harold Hyam Wingate Foundation.

Flush

by David Dipper

CHARLIE	ELLIOT COWAN
CUPID	BURN GORMAN
FRANCIS	DARREN TIGHE
HOLLY	CHRISTINE BOTTOMLEY
LILLY	KATHERINE PARKINSON

Director	Bijan Sheibani
Designer	Paul Burgess
Lighting Designer	Nigel Edwards
Sound Designer	John Leonard
Casting Director	Ginny Schiller
Fight Director	Paul Benzing

Production Manager	Nick Ferguson
Stage Manager	Marius Ronning
Stage Manager	Dani Youngman
Chief Technician	Nick Blount
Chief Electrician	Christoph Wagner
Lighting Technician	Ade Peterkin
Scenery built and painted by	Robert Knight Ltd.

Press Representation	Nancy Poole (020 7478 0142)
Photography	VCL/Antonio Mo/Getty Images
Production Photography	Andy Bradshaw

Soho Theatre and Writers' Centre
21 Dean St, London W1D 3NE

Admin: 020 7287 5060 *Fax:* 020 7287 5061 *Box Office:* 0870 429 6883
www.sohotheatre.com   *email:* box@sohotheatre.com

Biographies

Cast

Elliot Cowan
Charlie

Elliot's theatre credits include *The Seagull* (Edinburgh Festival); *Camille* (Lyric Hammersmith) and *Life of Galileo* (BAC, tour). Television credits include *The Project*, *Judge John Deed*, *Chillers* (BBC); *Jonathan Creek* (BBC1); *Crims* (Channel 4); *Foyle's War* (Greenlit Productions); *Ultimate Force* (Bentley Productions); *Rescue Me* (Tiger Aspect) and *It's a Girl Thing* (Optomen TV). Film credits include *Alexander* (Warner Brothers, dir. Oliver Stone) and *After Berlin* (dir. Richard Tovell).

Burn Gorman
Cupid

Burn's theatre credits include *Ladybird* (Royal Court); *American Street* (Paines Plough, Young Vic); *Tiny Dynamite* (Frantic Assembly, Paines Plough); *The Green Man* (Bush Theatre, Plymouth); *Ethel and Earnest* (Nottingham Playhouse); *Spilt Milk* (Young Vic); *Destination* (Riverside, Volcano); *Shooting Stars and Other Heavenly Pursuits* (Old Red Lion); *From Morning to Midnight* (ENO); *Traffic and Weather*, *Hidden Markings* (Contact Theatre); *Genius at Large* (LSO); *Underbetitled* (Royal Exchange Studio); *Seagulls*, *Princess Sharon* (Scarlet Theatre) and *Christmas Carol* (Tron Theatre). Television

credits include *The Shoreditch T**t* (Talkback Productions); *A Good Thief*, *Coronation Street* (Granada); *Mersey Beat* and *Casualty* (BBC). Film credits include *Colour Me Kubrick* and *Layercake*.

Darren Tighe
Francis

Darren's theatre credits include *Hunting for Dragons* (Soho Theatre); *The Backroom* (Soho Theatre, Bush Theatre); *Sweet Heart*, *Mojo* (Royal Court); *Summer Begins* (RNT Studio, Donmar Warehouse); *Precious* (West Yorkshire Playhouse); *Chimps* (Hampstead Theatre); *The Forest* (National Theatre). Television credits include *Silent Witness*, *Sally Phillip's Pilot*, *Crime and Punishment*, *Casualty*, *Dalziel and Pascoe*, *In Your Dreams*, *Hetty Wainthropp Investigates*, *All the King's Men* (BBC); *Foyle's War* (Greenlit); *M.I.T* (Thames); *Trust* (Box); *I Saw You, A & E*, *Cracker II*, *Medics*, *Band of Gold II* (Granada); *Rescue Me* and *Gimme, Gimme, Gimme* (Tiger Aspect). Film credits include *The Virgin of Liverpool* (Mob Film Company); *24 Hour Party People* (24 Hour Prod, Ltd); *High Heels Low Lifes* (High Heels Prods. Ltd); *More is Less* (TTO Limited); *Coming Down* (Kudos Productions); *Jude* (Obscure Films) and *Ill Communication* (Pilgrim Films).

Christine Bottomley
Holly

Christine's theatre credits include *Ladybird* (Royal Court); *New Writers' Workshop* (Royal Exchange) and *The Pleasureman* (Citizens Theatre). Television credits include *Early Doors, Grease Monkeys, Dalziel and Pascoe, Casualty, EastEnders, Inspector Lynley* (BBC). Film credits include *Untitled 03* (Thin Man Films).

Katherine Parkinson
Lilly

Katherine's theatre credits include *The Riot Act, The Increased Difficulty of Concentration* (Gate Theatre); *Camille* (Lyric Hammersmith); *Frame 312* (Donmar Warehouse); *Clytemnestra* (Oxford Playhouse); *Deep Throat Live On Stage* (Assembly Rooms, Edinburgh); and *The Age of Consent* (Bush Theatre and 2001 Edinburgh Festival).

Company

Bijan Sheibani
Director

Bijan's previous directing credits include *Party Time, One for the Road, The Stoning* (BAC); *The Clink* (The Rose Theatre); *Have I None* (Southwark Playhouse); *Summer* (Lion and Unicorn Theatre); *Peace for Our Time* (Cockpit Theatre); *Nightwatchman* (Oval Cricket Ground) and *The Lover* (Burton Taylor Theatre). Bijan won The James Menzies-Kitchin Memorial Trust Award for Young Directors 2003 and a Peter Brook Empty Space Award 2002. He is also the recipient of the 2004 Cohen Bursary at the National Theatre Studio and English Touring Theatre.

Paul Burgess
Designer

Paul trained at the Motley Theatre Design Course. Recent designs include *One for the Road, Party Time* (BAC); *Have I None* (Southwark Playhouse); *Peer Gynt* (Arcola) and *Choked* (Touring). Other designs include *Fred and Madge* (OUDS, Oxford Playhouse); *The People's Opera* (Touring); *Women and Criminals* (Here Arts Centre, New York) and *Sherlock Holmes* and *the Secret of Making Whoopee* (La Tea Theatre, New York). Assistant designing includes *The Ramayana* (RNT); *Ramayan Odyssey* (National Tour) and *Twelfth Night* (Shakespeare's

Globe US tour). He is currently Master of Properties and Hangings for the Globe's upcoming production of *Much Ado About Nothing*. In 2001 Paul co-founded Scale Project, a series of collaborations between visual artists and performers.

David Dipper
Writer

David wrote *Flush* at the age of 21 whilst a member of Soho Theatre's Young Writers' Group in 2003. He is currently working on a new full-length play, commissioned as part of Soho Theatre's Writers' Attachment Programme 2004.

Nigel Edwards
Lighting Designer

Nigel's theatre credits include *Dirty Butterfly* (Soho Theatre); *Some Confusions in the Law About Love, Bloody Mess, Club of No Regrets, Who Can Sing a Song to Unfrighten Me?, Speak Bitterness* (Forced Entertainment); *Clare de Luz* (Insomniac); *Cleansed, 4.48 Psychosis, Fallout, Ladybird* (The Royal Court); *Crave, Riddance, Sleeping Around, The Cosmonauts Last Message, Splendour* (Paines Plough); *One Minute, Arabian Night, The Boy Who Left Home* (ATC); *When Harry Met Sally* (Haymarket); *Sexual Perversity in Chicago* (The Comedy); *Roberto Zucco, The Mysteries, Shadows, The Tempest, Victoria* (RSC);

The Misanthrope (The Gate, Dublin); *Mr Heracles, Inconceivable* (West Yorkshire Playhouse); *Jenufa* (WNO); *Hansel and Gretel* (Opera North) and *Triumph of Love* (Almeida).

John Leonard
Sound Designer

John started work in theatre sound 30 years ago and during that time he has provided soundtracks for theatres all over the world. Recent productions for Soho Theatre include *Wrong Place, A Reckoning, Things You Shouldn't Say Past Midnight, Meeting Myself Coming Back* and *Kiss Me Like You Mean It*. Other recent productions include *The Dumb Waiter* (Oxford Playhouse); *Still Life/The Astonished Heart* – Double Bill, *The Entertainer* (Liverpool Everyman & Playhouse); *Les Liaisons Dangereuses* (West End); *Sweet Panic* (West End); *Absolutely! (Perhaps)* (West End); *Jumpers* (Royal National Theatre/West End); *The Master Builder* (Tour and West End); *Private Lives* (West End / Broadway); *Midnight's Children* (London, UK tour and USA); *Antony and Cleopatra* (RSC); *The Merry Wives of Windsor* (Ludlow Festival); *Sunday Father* (Hampstead); *Madame Tussaud's Exhibition* (New York, Amsterdam) and *Five Gold Rings, The Mercy Seat, I.D., The Lady from the Sea* (Almeida Theatre). John is a director of Aura Sound Design Ltd.

Soho Theatre Company

Soho is passionate in its commitment to new writing, producing a year-round programme of bold, original and accessible new plays – many of them from first-time playwrights.

'a foundry for new talent . . . one of the country's leading producers of new writing'   *Evening Standard*

Soho Theatre + Writers' Centre offers an invaluable resource to emerging playwrights. Our training and outreach programme includes the innovative Under 11's scheme, the Young Writers Group (15-25s) and a burgeoning series of Nuts and Bolts writing workshops designed to equip new writers with the basic tools of playwriting. We offer the nation's only unsolicited script-reading service, reporting on over 2,000 plays per year. We aim to develop and showcase the most promising new work through the national Verity Bargate Award, the Launch Pad scheme and the Writers' Attachment Programme, working to develop writers not just in theatre but also for TV and film.

'a creative hotbed . . . not only the making of theatre but the cradle for new screenplay and television scripts'   *The Times*

Contemporary, comfortable, air-conditioned and accessible, the Soho Theatre is busy from early morning to late at night. Alongside the production of new plays, it is also an intimate venue to see leading national and international comedians in an eclectic programme mixing emerging new talent with established names. Soho Theatre is home to Café Lazeez, serving delicious Indian fusion dishes downstairs with a lively bar upstairs that has a 1am license.

'London's coolest theatre by a mile'   *Midweek*

Soho Theatre Company is developing its work outside of the building, producing in Edinburgh and on tour in the UK whilst expanding the scope of its work with writers. It hosts the annual Soho Writers' Festival which brings together innovative practitioners from the creative industries with writers working in theatre, film, TV, radio, literature and poetry. Our programme aims to challenge, entertain and inspire writers and audiences from all backgrounds.

● soho
● theatre + writers' centre

21 Dean St
London W1D 3NE

Admin: 020 7287 5060
Box Office: 0870 429 6883
Minicom: 020 7478 0136
www.sohotheatre.com
email: box@sohotheatre.com

Bars and Restaurant

Café Lazeez brasserie serves Indian-fusion dishes
until 12 pm. Late bar open until 1am.
The Terrace Bar serves a range of soft and
alcoholic drinks.

Email information list

For regular programme updates and offers,
join our free email information list by emailing
box@sohotheatre.com or visiting
www.sohotheatre.com/mailing

If you would like to make any comments
about any of the productions seen at Soho Theatre,
visit our chatroom at www.sohotheatre.com

Hiring the theatre

Soho Theatre has a range of rooms and spaces
for hire. Please contact the theatre managers on
020 7287 5060
email hires@sohotheatre.com
or go to www.sohotheatre.com for further details.

Soho Theatre Company

Artistic Director: Abigail Morris
Acting Artistic Director:
    Jonathan Lloyd
Assistant to Artistic Director:
    Nadine Hoare
Administrative Producer:
    Mark Godfrey
Assistant to Administrative
    Producer: Tim Whitehead
Writers' Centre Director:
    Nina Steiger
Literary Assistant: David Lane
Casting Director: Ginny Schiller
Marketing and Development
    Director: Zoe Reed
Development Manager:
    Gayle Rogers
Marketing Officer: Jenni Wardle
Marketing and Development
    Assistant: Kelly Duffy
Press Officer: Nancy Poole
    (020 7478 0142)
General Manager:
    Catherine Thornborrow
Front of House and Building
    Manager: Julia Christie
Financial Controller: Kevin Dunn
Book Keeper: Elva Tehan
Box Office Manager:
    Kate Truefitt
Deputy Box Office Manager:
    Steve Lock
Box Office Assistant:
    Janice Draper, Jennie Fellows,
    Richard Gay, Leah Read,
    Will Sherriff Hammond,
    Harriet Spencer, Natalie Worrall
Duty Managers: Mike Owen,
    Rebecca Storey, Miranda Yates
    and Peter Youthed.
Front of House staff:
    Rachel Bavidge, Louise Beere,
    Helene Le Bohec, Sharon
    Degan, Colin Goodwin,
    Matthew Halpin, Siobhan
    Hyams, Grethe Jensen,
    Minho Kwon, Carole Menduni,
    Katherine Smith, Rachel
    Southern, Maya Symeou, Luke
    Tebbutt and Jamie Zubairi
Production Manager:
    Nick Ferguson
Chief Technician: Nick Blount
Chief Lighting Technician:
    Christoph Wagner
Lighting Technician: Ade Peterkin

Board of Directors (*) and Members of the Company

Nicholas Allott*
David Aukin – chair
Lisa Bryer
Tony Buckley
Sophie Clarke-Jervoise
Cllr Robert Davis
Tony Elliott*
Barbara Follett MP*
Norma Heyman*
Bruce Hyman
Lynne Kirwin
Tony Marchant
Michael Naughton*
David Pelham*
Michael Pennington
Sue Robertson*
Philippe Sands
Eric H Senat*
Meera Syal
Marc Vlessing*
Zoë Wanamaker
Sir Douglas Wass
Richard Wilson OBE*
Roger Wingate*

Honorary Patrons

Bob Hoskins *president*
Peter Brook CBE
Simon Callow
Sir Richard Eyre

Development Committee

Bruce Hyman – *chair*
Nicholas Allott
David Aukin
Don Black OBE
David Day
Catherine Fehler
Nigel Gee
Madeleine Hamel
Marie Helvin
Norma Heyman
Cathy Ingram
Carol Jackson
Roger Jospé
Lise Mayer
Patricia McGowan
Michael Naughton
Jane O'Donald
Marc Sands
Philippe Sands
Barbara Stone
Des Violaris
Richard Wilson OBE
Jeremy Zimmerman

The Soho Theatre Development Campaign

Soho Theatre Company receives core funding from Arts
Council England, London and Westminster City Council. In
order to provide as diverse a programme as possible and
expand our audience development and outreach work, we rely
upon additional support from trusts, foundations, individuals
and businesses.

All of our major sponsors share a common commitment to
developing new areas of activity and encouraging creative
partnerships between business and the arts.

We are immensely grateful for the invaluable support from
our sponsors and donors and wish to thank them for their
continued commitment.

Soho Theatre Company has launched a new Friends Scheme
to support its work in developing new writers and reaching
new audiences. To find out how to become a Friend of Soho
Theatre and what you will receive in return, contact the
development department on 020 7478 0111, email
development@sohotheatre.com or visit www.sohotheatre.com

SPONSORS

Angels Costumiers, Arts & Business,
Bloomberg, Getty Images, TBWA\GGT

Major Supporters Calouste Gulbenkian Foundation • The
Foyle Foundation • The Paul Hamlyn Foundation • Roger and
Cecil Jospé • John Lyon's Charity • The Wellcome Trust •
The Garfield Weston Foundation • The Harold Hyam Wingate
Foundation • Roger Wingate

Education Patrons Tony and Rita Gallagher • Nigel Gee •
Jack and Linda Keenan

Trusts and Foundations Anon • Sidney and Elizabeth Corob
Charitable Trust • Delfont Foundation • The Follett Trust •
JG Hogg Charitable Trust • Hyde Park Place Estate Charity •
John Lewis, Oxford Street • Linbury Trust • The Mackintosh
Foundation • The Moose Foundation for the Arts •
The St James' Trust • The Kobler Trust • Tesco Charity Trust •
The Hazel Wood Charitable Trust

Dear Friends Madeleine Hamel • Richard and Diana Toeman •
Jill and Michael Barrington • SoFie and Le'le'

Friends Thank you also to the many Soho Friends we are
unable to list here. For a full list of our patrons please visit
www.sohotheatre.com

FLUSH

David Dipper

For Helena

Acknowledgements

My thanks to Jonathan Lloyd, Nina Steiger and everyone at the Soho Theatre. Also, Jonathan Lichenstein, Charlotte Mann and Tessa Walker.

Special thanks to my parents for their unflinching support.

D.D.

6

Characters

LILLY

FRANCIS

CHARLIE

CUPID

HOLLY

Scene One

LILLY *enters with a shoulder bag and a poster tube.*

FRANCIS. Hello.

LILLY. Sorry. Hello. I'm Lilly, Charlie's sister.

FRANCIS. Hi.

LILLY. I'm sorry. I didn't mean to wake you.

FRANCIS. Oh don't worry.

LILLY. You're Francis?

FRANCIS. Yeah sorry, Francis, yeah.

   Beat.

LILLY. You did know I was coming today?

FRANCIS. Yes.

   Beat.

LILLY. Thanks for putting me up like this.

FRANCIS. Don't worry. Landlord's been trying to fill that
   room for ages.

LILLY. That's surprising.

FRANCIS. Yeah I know, it's a shit-hole.

   Beat.

   Is that all your stuff?

LILLY. Yeah. Well not really. I can pop home for anything else
   I need.

FRANCIS. Right.

   Beat.

LILLY. What's with the cards?

FRANCIS. Oh, I was going through hands, possibilities. Must have dozed off.

LILLY. Do you fancy a game?

FRANCIS. What, poker?

LILLY. Yeah.

FRANCIS. You play poker?

LILLY. Yeah.

FRANCIS. What kind?

LILLY. Texas Hold'em, mostly. You?

FRANCIS. Yeah, Texas Hold'em.

LILLY. Fancy a couple of rounds?

FRANCIS. Now?

LILLY. Yeah, why not?

Beat.

FRANCIS. I play with money.

LILLY *smiles.*

LILLY. That's fine.

Beat.

Come on. Don't be scared.

FRANCIS. I'd feel a bit weird taking your money.

LILLY. Don't worry, that won't happen.

FRANCIS. Did Charlie teach you how to play?

LILLY. Yes.

FRANCIS. I reckon you're in quite a lot of trouble then.

They sit at the poker table.

LILLY. I'll tell him you said that.

FRANCIS smiles and deals. He looks at LILLY and his smile fades.

FRANCIS. She died a year ago today on a morning of overcast grey and sleet.

And everyone's fucking sorry.

So her dad writes a poem and he reads it at the funeral, but it's shit, 'cause he works in a bank.

I meet her family for the first time after. Lovely service, yeah, all that. We go back to her house for the most miserable sandwiches I've ever seen. And her nan's pretty cut up. But I'm fine. And they show me her room with all the tokens of success. Certificates, head-girl tie pinned on the wall, fucking ballet photos, prom photos of her in a ballgown, smiling next to some tuxed-up prick who in five years' time will date rape some fifteen-year-old and no-one will be surprised. Lilly's little sister is twelve and she cries over some miserable lipstick that she had given her at some memorable fucking occasion that no-one can fucking remember.

I say goodbye to Charlie and he's barely holding it together in his old black suit bought for special occasions such as christenings and his sister's funeral.

They told me to stay in touch and sent me a Christmas card. I didn't have the heart to tell them that I can't stand their daughter. I didn't have the heart to tell them that the world is a better place without that arrogant fucking princess parading her stupid fucking axioms for life. She sent me a text message asking if I was missing her lots. I don't miss you at all, my darling.

LILLY. I missed you.

FRANCIS. Did you have a good night?

LILLY. No, not really. We spent the evening with these Cypriot guys.

FRANCIS (*directed at* LILLY). She always talks about men she's met with, usually foreign, and she never bets before the flop, stupid cow.

LILLY. I only spent five quid. They bought us everything.

FRANCIS. I exaggerate my involvement with any girl that comes to mind. Scan for jealousy. Raise her three.

LILLY. You're never going to believe it but that Greek guy who fancies me was there.

FRANCIS. She calls and raises another three, thinking she's won.

LILLY. I think he's following me.

FRANCIS. I don't take the bait.

Pause.

LILLY. I'm sorry about the other night. Raise ten.

Beat.

FRANCIS. What are you sorry for?

LILLY. I don't know, I'm just embarrassed for you.

Beat.

FRANCIS. Don't be, I was drunk and horny. Raise five.

LILLY. Apparently not that horny. Raise ten.

Beat.

I'm sorry, I won't mention it again. I just thought it was so funny, couldn't stop laughing. Are you seeing my raise?

Beat.

FRANCIS. Yeah.

Beat.

What do you have?

LILLY. What do you have?

FRANCIS. Three of a kind.

FRANCIS *lays down his hand.*

LILLY. With a jack.

FRANCIS. What about you?

LILLY *lays down her hand.*

LILLY. Three of a kind with a king.

LILLY *rakes in the money.*

Unlucky, Romeo.

FRANCIS. I'm going to bed.

FRANCIS *leaves.*

Scene Two

CHARLIE. So I'm a coke addict. I'm a fag. I was abused as a child. I'm a recovering alcoholic. I like to rape women. I tried to kill myself once but there was no fucking through trains. Don't ask me about the last fight I was in. No, I've never put anyone in hospital, nudge, nudge, wink, wink, mine's a pint. Grew up on a council estate. My dad drives an Aston. I would be in the SAS but I got a dodgy ankle. My mate's in the SAS. My brother's going to be the next Basement Jaxx. These shoes? Gucci. I'd do anything for my son. You watching the match tonight?

CUPID *enters.*

CUPID. So I'm sitting having a beer with my mate so he doesn't remember his sister's dead except I'm drinking JD 'cause the smell of beer reminds me of when my dad tried to fuck me. Nah, I'm kidding.

CHARLIE (*to* CUPID). It's fucking rotten but clever: she walks in and starts sucking off this old fat guy while he's sitting on the toilet. Now you know me, Cupy, old fat guys don't really float my boat but this scene drives me fucking crazy.

CUPID. He's talking about this bit in the *Dirty Anal Kelly* series where the eponymous girly, who is widely suspected of being a bit of a retard, sucks off an old . . . well, you heard the story. Charlie's pretty stupid but he knows about porn, and on any other day I could listen to him talk bullshit for hours but today I'm off with the fairies.

CHARLIE. You get some attractive girl to fuck some guy with a big cock, she screams, he comes all over her tits, you get your wank, porno guy gets his twenty quid, your bird gets the night off, everybody's happy. But in this scene she sucked off an old fat guy on a toilet which is problematic at first but ultimately fucking simple.

Slight pause.

CUPID. Yeah?

CHARLIE. Yeah, 'cause it's like they're pointing at you and saying 'this girl would fuck you if you met her, she's fucking this old guy – you could have her' and I'm like all 'what, me?' and they're going 'yeah, fuck her however you want' and it drives me crazy.

CUPID. So there's two of us in this room and Charlie's sister's semiconscious on the bed, and because she's pissed, her skirt, which was too fucking short anyway, is like up around her stomach and both of us are thinking the same thing and the air is fucking electric.

Scene Three

HOLLY *and* FRANCIS *are sitting at the poker table.*

HOLLY. At the same time at the other end of town.

FRANCIS. The dealer deals three community cards called 'the flop'. Now if you're sitting on, say, two hearts and two more come out in the flop, you're 3–1 against on drawing a flush on the final two cards.

HOLLY. He can't sustain an erection so he teaches me stuff in case I notice it's getting late.

FRANCIS. If you're new to the game, most people will see four suited cards and pile all their money in but two times out of three, you're going to lose.

HOLLY. We used to try all the time but I've found that he gets horny when I don't want it and then loses it when I do, think it's the pressure, so I'm trying a new approach of permanently pretending that I don't want it. Blowjobs are fine mostly.

FRANCIS. Are you listening to me?

HOLLY. Course I am.

FRANCIS. What did I just say?

HOLLY. You were talking about the odds on getting a flush on the last couple of cards.

FRANCIS. Drawing a flush.

HOLLY. Yeah.

Beat.

FRANCIS. If you don't want to learn, I don't mind.

HOLLY. I do want to learn.

FRANCIS. But if you don't, just say.

HOLLY. I do want to.

FRANCIS. Okay but you're going to have to listen.

HOLLY. I was listening.

FRANCIS. No, that's fine. I'm just saying that if you want to learn, then you have to listen to me because it's not easy.

HOLLY. Francis, I'm listening.

Beat.

FRANCIS. We always play cards before we go to bed to stop her having nightmares, which is, you know, pretty mental. Do you want to try a round?

HOLLY. As long as you don't hate me when I win.

FRANCIS. So we play and she wins and I hate her.

HOLLY. You said not to wait until the final two cards to draw a flush.

FRANCIS. I said that you can, but two times out of three, you'll lose.

HOLLY. But I won.

FRANCIS. But two times out of three, you'll lose.

HOLLY. But in that instance, I won.

FRANCIS. Yes.

HOLLY. So in that instance, I was right to do that.

FRANCIS. No.

HOLLY. But I won.

FRANCIS. Yes but two times out of three, you would have lost.

HOLLY. But this time I won.

FRANCIS. Yes.

HOLLY. So in this specific instance, I was right.

FRANCIS. No, because every three rounds you play like that, you'll lose two of them.

HOLLY. Okay, but this time, I bet my money and I won, so what I'm saying is, in this instance, I was right.

FRANCIS. You don't understand.

HOLLY. I'm not playing with you anymore.

FRANCIS. Why not?

HOLLY. 'Cause you hate me when I win.

FRANCIS. Oh, do me a favour. It's your turn to deal.

FRANCIS *bangs down the cards on the table.*

HOLLY. Fine.

FRANCIS. So we play and she wins and I hate her.

Scene Four

FRANCIS *and* CUPID *sit at the poker table.*

Long silence.

FRANCIS. Did you get home alright?

CUPID *looks at* FRANCIS.

Beat.

CUPID. Yeah.

Beat.

Don't remember much.

Pause.

I thought Charlie was coming.

FRANCIS. He's late.

CUPID. I know he's late.

FRANCIS. So there's two reasons why Cupid's tense, only, one reason he doesn't give a shit about, and when she comes in I don't give anything away.

Scene Five

FRANCIS *and* LILLY *sit at the poker table.*

They play poker in silence.

FRANCIS. Have a good night?

LILLY. Yes. You?

FRANCIS. It was alright.

Beat.

LILLY. Did you have a game?

FRANCIS. Yeah. How did you know?

LILLY. I didn't.

Beat.

Did you win?

FRANCIS. Yeah.

LILLY. How much?

FRANCIS. Hundred.

LILLY. Really? A hundred quid?

Beat.

FRANCIS. Cupid was there.

LILLY. Yeah?

Beat.

Did my name come up?

FRANCIS. No, not at all.

LILLY. Oh.

FRANCIS. Why would it?

LILLY. Don't know. Just wondered.

Silence.

FRANCIS. Where did you go tonight?

LILLY. Jacks.

FRANCIS. Yeah?

LILLY. Yeah.

FRANCIS. What time did you leave?

LILLY. I don't know. About half an hour ago. It was closing.

FRANCIS. I went to Jacks after the game, I didn't see you.

LILLY. We didn't get there until late.

FRANCIS. What time?

Beat.

LILLY. Elevenish.

FRANCIS. I was there at eleven.

LILLY. Maybe a bit later.

FRANCIS. I left at one.

LILLY. Probably just didn't see each other.

FRANCIS. That's strange, don't you think?

Beat.

How come you didn't go in school uniform?

Beat.

LILLY. It wasn't 'school disco' tonight, that's on Thursdays.

LILLY *suppresses a smile.*

FRANCIS. You're lying.

LILLY. I'm not.

FRANCIS. I can tell.

LILLY. You can't tell.

Beat.

FRANCIS. Cupid left early tonight. Said he's seeing this bird he's got on the go.

LILLY. Yeah?

FRANCIS. Really young and desperate, he said. Charlie laughed his arse off.

Beat.

LILLY. So?

FRANCIS. Nice arse, rotten eczema he said. Remind you of anyone?

LILLY. I'm flattered you think I've got a nice arse but –

FRANCIS. You're fucking Cupid.

Beat.

LILLY. Yeah I am.

Beat.

Does that bother you?

FRANCIS. No.

Scene Six

CUPID, CHARLIE *and* FRANCIS *are playing poker.*

CUPID. Back in the present. Just before the end of the play.

CHARLIE. You spending the evening with your girly tonight, Franny?

FRANCIS. Yeah.

Beat.

CHARLIE. What, you going round hers?

FRANCIS. No, mine probably.

CHARLIE. Oh okay.

Beat.

Let me know if you two split up. I'd like to see if she's how I remember.

FRANCIS. No problem. I'll get her to call you.

CHARLIE. Yeah, I wonder if she's still as shit.

Pause.

Yeah, she was really shit.

Pause.

'Cause I fucked her and she was shit.

FRANCIS. Did someone tell you that you were good at this, Charlie?

CHARLIE. Good at what?

Beat.

I don't know what you're talking about mate.

Just making conversation.

Silence.

What about you, Cupy?

CUPID. I don't have a girlfriend.

CHARLIE. Well if you spent less time sucking cocks . . .

CUPID *looks at* CHARLIE.

CUPID. What did you say?

FRANCIS. I look at Cupid, Cupid looks at Charlie and Charlie looks at the flop 'cause he's got a shit hand.

CHARLIE. I said you shouldn't suck so many cocks.

Slight pause.

CUPID. That's pretty funny, Charlie.

CUPID *looks at his hand.*

FRANCIS. Cupid steps back from the ledge, I shit my pants and Charlie doesn't know what the fuck just happened.

CHARLIE. So I'm tapping this fat bird, real fucking fat, beef burger tits, the lot, and she's monster desperate being so fucking fat so I tell her I love her but I don't, in fact I did that with my last girlfriend too. I think I'm into the grass is always greener and all that shit. Anyway, she lives in this flat and every time I go round there her friend is standing outside smoking and we talk and she's pretty interesting and I really want her, really fucking want her. Couple of nights later I'm in this club and she comes up and starts dancing with me, real dirty. Then she whispers to me 'are you into anal sex?' and I go 'what once a year?' and she laughs 'cause she thinks I'm a funny prick. So we're in her room getting down to it, but nothing happens. Never happened before, you know, usually I'm as hard as . . . well you know, I'm usually pretty fucking hard, but this one time, nothing happens. She says don't worry and all that shit and I'm feeling like a right useless twat and we fall asleep. Next thing I know my phone's ringing and it's Tiff and I look at the clock and it's like six in the morning and she's all like 'where the fuck are you?' and I'm all like 'I'm fucking your best friend' and she laughs, 'cause she knows I'm a flippant son of a bitch but I hang up 'cause I've got an absolute stonker on. So I start getting dirty again with this girl and when she wakes up, she's feeling pretty horny too. So we start, but it's a pump-pump-squirt job and she's all like 'what the fuck was that?' and I'm embarrassed but I know I've still got the high-ground 'cause I fucked her up the arse and I tell her that and she shuts up.

CUPID. Okay I'm in this bar in Aylesbury and I'm shitting it 'cause this far out of the M25 it's a different beast and I meet this girl who hates cigarettes but doesn't mind putting just about anyone's dick in her mouth. So I highlight this incongruity but she fails to see the irony or the paradox or the whatever the fuck it is I'm trying to make her see. Anyway, she sucks my dick and to be honest she's not that good, so I go home with this girl who assures me she's not a midget. And when I fuck her I think of that bird from *Harry Potter* which is, you know, pretty sick but understandable.

CHARLIE. Right, so I'm just about to go to this fancy-dress party and I'm all dressed up like an SS guard when this bird I know calls, asking if I wanted to come round, keep her company. So I wash my cock and go round there but she's having none of it, so I bend her over her kid's Tomy playhouse and do her and she's all like screaming and crying and shit so I pick her up and smash her head against the wall and there's blood everywhere and she's laying on the floor and I'm fucked 'cause this costume's hired and I think all I need now is some anorexic kid watching and I'm living the dream.

CUPID. Okay, there's two of us in this room and this girl is semiconscious on the bed –

FRANCIS. Shut up, Cupid.

CUPID *and* CHARLIE *look at* FRANCIS.

Beat.

CUPID. Don't worry, Francis, it's fine.

FRANCIS. You're not funny.

CUPID. I'm not trying to be funny, Francis, I'm trying to tell my mate a story.

FRANCIS. Don't do it, Cupid.

CHARLIE. Don't do what?

Would someone care to tell me what the fuck's going on?

CUPID. Francis, relax.

FRANCIS. You want to do this now?

Beat.

Scene Seven

FRANCIS *is playing cards with* LILLY.

LILLY. Okay, I've just come back from netball so I'm still in the short skirt and shit and I'm standing there cutting bread. Anyway, Cupid comes in but I don't hear him and he grabs me from behind, and without even saying anything he starts to fuck me, really hard.

FRANCIS. I don't want to hear this, Lilly.

LILLY. Okay, I'll just tell you this bit. So he's fucking me really hard and he's got my hands pinned to the work surface and when I look down it looks like he's got the knife in his hand and it sends me wild. Is that fucked up?

FRANCIS. Yes.

LILLY. Piss off it's not, it's adventurous, he's fantastic.

FRANCIS. Where do you think he is tonight?

LILLY. I know where he is. He's gone to see his mum for a couple of days.

Silence.

We're thinking of going on holiday together.

FRANCIS. What, he's asked you, has he?

LILLY. Yes.

FRANCIS. What, he's actually asked you?

LILLY. Well he's talked about a holiday.

Silence.

He loves me you know.

FRANCIS. No he doesn't, Lilly.

LILLY. He does, he doesn't have to say it.

FRANCIS. He's never even mentioned you.

LILLY. Well he can't, not while Charlie's there.

FRANCIS. I don't know why, but it surprises me that you're so stupid.

LILLY. I think you're jealous.

FRANCIS. Yeah right.

LILLY. I don't think you can bear it that Cupid comes over here every night and fucks me. Raise ten.

FRANCIS. I think you overestimate what you mean to me, Lilly.

LILLY. I'm sorry you have to listen, I try and keep quiet. Actually, make it twenty. Raise twenty.

Slight pause.

You should give me more credit you know.

FRANCIS. Right.

LILLY. I do know what I'm doing.

FRANCIS. Right.

Beat.

LILLY. Anyway, Cupid wouldn't screw me around. He knows what Charlie would do to him.

FRANCIS. You think Cupid's scared of Charlie?

LILLY. Course he is.

FRANCIS. Do you think Cupid would be holding you down and fucking you in the kitchen if he was scared of Charlie?

LILLY. You know what, I hate it when I tell you something and you use it against me in an argument.

FRANCIS. I didn't realise we were having an argument.

LILLY. You can be such a cock sometimes.

Silence.

You can really piss me off when you want to, do you know that?

Silence.

Oh what, you're sulking now, is that it?

FRANCIS. Fuck off, Lilly.

LILLY. You fuck off.

FRANCIS. You're such a stupid little cow. You don't have a clue.

LILLY. Yeah right, like I don't understand, like I can't see exactly what you're doing.

FRANCIS. Oh really, what is it I'm doing?

LILLY. What, you want me to say it?

Beat.

FRANCIS. I'm sick of this.

FRANCIS *stands up.*

LILLY. We're in the middle of a round.

Can we please have a game that doesn't end with you walking out?

FRANCIS *leaves*.

Scene Eight

CHARLIE *is sitting on the sofa*.

Pause.

FRANCIS *enters*.

CHARLIE *rises*.

CHARLIE. Alright Franny, take a seat.

FRANCIS. You wanted to speak to me?

CHARLIE. Yes, what it is is that I've got this mate who owes me a couple of favours so he gets me quality, cheap gear. You interested?

FRANCIS. No thanks Charlie.

CHARLIE. I got Rohypnol, Ritalin, you know, just the trendy shit. You interested?

FRANCIS. No Charlie, I'm not.

CHARLIE. I mean you're a good kid Franny, I'm sure I could do you a competitive deal.

FRANCIS. Right, I got to go.

CHARLIE. Okay, me too. I can't hang around, I have to go and see some unlucky prick down on Edgware.

FRANCIS. Right.

CHARLIE. He's gonna wish he hadn't fucked me around this week.

FRANCIS. Okay, I'll see you around.

CHARLIE. I'll probably have to put a bat to his legs, the stupid fucker.

FRANCIS. Right.

CHARLIE. Wife and kids probably be there screaming but I don't fucking care. I've got a job to do.

FRANCIS. Okay, I'll see you around.

At another part of the stage, HOLLY *is sitting.*

CUPID *enters and stops.*

Pause.

CUPID. Are you Francis's girlfriend?

HOLLY. Yeah, sorry you are?

CUPID. I'm Cupid.

HOLLY. Cupid? What a great name.

CUPID. Thank you.

HOLLY. How did you know?

CUPID. Don't know, sensed it.

HOLLY. You psychic?

CUPID. Yeah, maybe I am.

Beat.

HOLLY. So how do you know Francis?

Beat.

CUPID. We play poker together.

HOLLY. You must be rich.

CUPID. I don't know what he's told you but he's actually pretty shit.

HOLLY. That's what I mean.

CUPID. Oh right, yeah.

Slight pause.

He's going to be quite a long time, they're talking business.

HOLLY. Oh, Francis said it wouldn't take long.

CUPID. Well Charlie isn't the easiest person to get away from.

HOLLY. What do you mean 'business'?

CUPID. You know, this and that. Do you want to go for a drink while you're waiting?

CHARLIE. I mean I've given him a chance to pay and he didn't so you know, I've got to deal with it. It's really a discipline problem.

FRANCIS. Okay, I'll see you around.

CHARLIE. Someone like you would think, you know, twenty quid, it's not enough to break a man's legs but you're wrong. I can't let people think I'm a soft touch.

FRANCIS. Right.

CHARLIE. I've done it for less too. One guy only owed me a tenner, which to some people is a lot of money but to me, you know, I don't even notice it. Still did him.

FRANCIS. Okay, I'll see you around.

CHARLIE. Or there was the Chink geezer only owed me a quid. He goes 'look mate, is only a quid.' I go 'firstly, you ain't my mate and secondly, you can't come down here and turn round and say to me it's only quid 'cause, you know, at the end of the day, it's my quid.' He shut up, I knocked him sparco, then went to work on him.

FRANCIS. Right.

CUPID. There's a coffee shop round the corner.

HOLLY. No, I should really wait for Francis.

CUPID. Okay.

Beat.

So what is it you do, Holly?

HOLLY. I'm a student.

CUPID. No, I mean what do you study?

HOLLY. Psychology.

CUPID. Is that why you're going out with Francis?

HOLLY. Francis doesn't do Psychology.

CUPID. Oh right.

Interesting?

HOLLY. Yeah.

CUPID. So why did I never want to fuck my mother?

HOLLY. Because you're a pervert.

CUPID *laughs.*

CUPID. You know what, there's probably some truth in that.

CHARLIE. One geezer didn't owe me anything. I still put him in Harold Wood for three weeks.

FRANCIS. Okay, I'll see you around.

CHARLIE. Wife and kids were screaming, begging me to stop, but you know, what do they expect me to do about it?

FRANCIS. Right.

CHARLIE. Grandparents were there, going mental.

FRANCIS. Okay, I'll see you around.

CHARLIE. And the grandparents had friends round. Really old friends, known each other for twenty years or something, from the war. They were screaming and shouting too.

FRANCIS. Right.

CHARLIE. And they were going to me 'you can't do this to someone in church' and I go 'well I don't believe in God so what the fuck do I care.' 'Cause this geezer was in church at the time.

FRANCIS. Okay, I'll see you around.

CUPID. You look really familiar.

HOLLY. Right.

CUPID. You do.

HOLLY. Right.

CUPID. I'm serious, it's your face.

HOLLY. Does this usually work?

CUPID. I'm serious.

HOLLY. Well, I'm really sorry but I don't remember you.

CUPID. Maybe you don't recognise me with my clothes on.

HOLLY. I'm pretty sure I'd remember.

CUPID. Actually, you're right. You would.

CHARLIE. So this copper comes up and tries to pull me off
    him and I go 'look copper, this piece of shit's been trying to
    stop me making a living, I'm just doing my fucking job' and
    this copper goes 'fair enough mate, that's reasonable' and
    leaves me alone.

FRANCIS. Right.

CHARLIE. 'Cause see coppers understand that. When I was in
    the force I had to arrest scum like me all the time. Some
    lowlife pricks, real shits of the earth.

FRANCIS. Okay, I'll see you around.

CHARLIE. I had to arrest rapists, gangsters, murderers,
    nonces, the lot and I wanted to cut their bollocks off with
    wire-cutters 'cause, you know, I'm a decent bloke but that's
    not what the job is.

FRANCIS. Right.

CHARLIE. You just have to step back which was easy for
    me 'cause I'm a pacifist and I know that violence is self-
    perpetuating.

FRANCIS. Okay, I'll see you around.

CHARLIE. But the young guns that you pull in get their heads down and clock some poor twat in a bar, 'cause they've got a small prick and I've got a big prick so I can't.

FRANCIS. Right.

HOLLY *is showing the screen of her phone to* CUPID *while he types in a number to his phone.*

CUPID. Okay, I'll text you or something.

HOLLY. Okay.

CUPID. I'll try not to do it when Francis is in.

HOLLY. What an odd thing to say.

CUPID. I just know what Francis is like, wouldn't want to 'cause a problem.

HOLLY. That's not what he's like.

CUPID. You must know a different side to him.

HOLLY. Yeah, I must.

Beat.

So you and Francis are mates then?

Beat.

CUPID. We play cards.

HOLLY. Okay.

CUPID. You get to know someone pretty well if you play them enough.

HOLLY. I see.

CUPID. I don't know that we would say we were mates though. Why? What's he told you?

HOLLY. Nothing.

CUPID. No, we just play cards.

CHARLIE. I used to pick 'em up in this piece-of-shit council estate where their dad had been slapping their mum around

all their life and they had to watch. And the mum is
addicted to crack and died like a week after she's had 'em.

FRANCIS. Okay, I'll see you around.

CHARLIE. So they don't go through the Oedipus complex
where they want to fuck their mother and kill their father
and that's why they grow up to be poofs. Actually I tell
a lie, they do want to kill their old man, 'cause he's been
knocking around their mum who's dead.

FRANCIS. Right.

CHARLIE. I mean I'm not saying I'm a saint. I'm not. You've
never seen me in a bad mood. Good fucking thing too, but
you know, I know how to control it.

FRANCIS. Okay, I'll see you around.

CHARLIE. I mean I thought I was going to kill someone last
week. I was in this club, dancing and this girl comes over
to me and goes 'I really want your cock in my mouth',
yeah, couldn't believe it. Turns out she's a prostitute on a
busman's holiday. So I buy her a few drinks before I take
her round the back and fuck her and she's all like 'fuck me,
you've got a huge prick' and she's really into it. Then she
turns round and charges me a ton. And I go 'no way, you
loved it, you know, you should be paying me'. And she goes
'give me my money' and I go 'no, I'm not paying', and she
goes 'you fucking are' and I go 'I'm fucking not, verbal
contract innit'. Anyway, cut a long story short, her pimp
comes along, kicks the shit out of me and nicks my wallet.
But I tell you what, when I woke up in hospital I went
absolutely mental.

FRANCIS *exits.*

Anyway I better go.

FRANCIS. Cupid, what are you doing here?

CUPID. Sorting out a few things.

FRANCIS (*to* HOLLY). You ready to go?

HOLLY. Sure. It was nice to meet you.

CUPID. Yeah, you too Holly. Good luck with all your stuff.

HOLLY. Thanks, you too.

CUPID. Who does your girlfriend remind me of, Francis?

FRANCIS. I don't know, Cupid. We got to go.

   CHARLIE *enters.*

CUPID. Charlie, who does Holly remind you of?

   CHARLIE *looks at* HOLLY.

   Silence.

FRANCIS. This is Charlie. Charlie, this is my girlfriend Holly.

   Silence.

Scene Nine

Music is playing loudly in another room.

FRANCIS. At a party. We've had a few.

   FRANCIS *and* CUPID *begin to kiss and begin to undress each other.*

CUPID. Did you lock the door?

FRANCIS. Yes.

   CUPID *goes down on* FRANCIS.

CUPID. Did you know one of the Krays had a gay relationship?

FRANCIS. No, I didn't know that.

Scene Ten

FRANCIS *is asleep on the sofa.*

HOLLY *enters and turns on the lamp.*

FRANCIS *wakes up with a start.*

HOLLY. You okay?

FRANCIS. Yeah.

  What time is it?

HOLLY. About six.

FRANCIS. Oh thank fuck for that.

HOLLY. What?

FRANCIS. Oh nothing, decent telly.

HOLLY. You playing poker tonight?

FRANCIS. Yeah, why?

HOLLY. Just wondered.

FRANCIS. What about you?

HOLLY. Going out.

FRANCIS. Where are you going?

HOLLY. Don't know, some club I suppose.

FRANCIS. Do you want me to come?

HOLLY. You can't.

FRANCIS. I can.

HOLLY. You've got a game.

FRANCIS. I can miss it. I don't mind.

HOLLY. No, it's fine.

FRANCIS. Who's going?

HOLLY. Just a few of us.

FRANCIS. What, uni friends?

HOLLY. Yes.

FRANCIS. I can miss the game. I don't mind.

HOLLY. No, it's fine.

Beat.

FRANCIS. Can you ask them if they want another game?

HOLLY. Okay.

FRANCIS. Will you remember?

HOLLY. Yes.

FRANCIS. Do you promise?

HOLLY. Francis, I said I'd remember.

Beat.

FRANCIS. What time will you be back?

HOLLY. Late.

FRANCIS. She asked me to teach her poker, but I knew she'd be too fucking good at it.

HOLLY. I better get ready.

HOLLY *exits.*

FRANCIS. But I teach her anyway, and she is too fucking good at it.

FRANCIS *starts playing with a pack of cards.*

HOLLY *enters.*

HOLLY. You waiting up for me?

FRANCIS. No. Have fun?

HOLLY. Yes. What you doing?

FRANCIS. Thinking through hands, possibilities.

HOLLY. Did you win?

FRANCIS. Yeah.

HOLLY. How much?

FRANCIS. Hundred quid.

HOLLY. Well done.

FRANCIS. Thanks. Where did you go?

HOLLY. Are you lying?

FRANCIS. Yeah.

HOLLY. How much did you lose?

FRANCIS. Hundred quid.

HOLLY. Expensive.

FRANCIS. Yeah. What about you?

HOLLY. What about me what?

FRANCIS. Did you . . . spend a lot of money?

HOLLY. Are you still lying to me?

FRANCIS. No.

   Beat.

   Yes.

HOLLY. I didn't spend much, people bought me drinks.

FRANCIS. Really? Who?

HOLLY. Oh you know, friends.

FRANCIS. What, blokes?

HOLLY. Yeah, so what?

FRANCIS. Nothing, just wondered. Cupid got your text message, thought it was very funny.

HOLLY. Oh right. I was replying to one he sent me.

FRANCIS. Oh right.

HOLLY. Do you want to play poker?

FRANCIS. You know, if the universe is infinite then somewhere there's a place where Holly is taking it from Cupid.

No thanks.

HOLLY. Just a couple of hands?

FRANCIS. No, I'm a bit sick of it.

HOLLY. Is that because you always lose?

FRANCIS. Yeah.

HOLLY. No, I mean is that because you always lose to me?

FRANCIS. Yeah.

Beat.

HOLLY. You okay?

FRANCIS. Yeah, I'm fine.

Beat.

HOLLY. You know, I wish you'd talk to me when you're feeling shit.

FRANCIS. I see the bluff a mile away.

It's nothing, I'm fine.

Scene Eleven

FRANCIS. Earlier that evening. Where's Charlie?

CUPID. He's late. Do you want to start without him?

Beat.

FRANCIS. Sure.

They begin.

CUPID. How's Holly?

FRANCIS. She's fine.

CUPID. Did she get my text message?

FRANCIS. Yes. Did you get her reply?

CUPID. Yes, very funny.

FRANCIS. I'll pass that on for you.

CUPID. No, don't worry, I'll tell her myself.

FRANCIS. Great.

CUPID. Raise ten.

FRANCIS. Fold.

CUPID. Clever boy.

FRANCIS. I've had better set-ups from Charlie.

CUPID. I wasn't setting you up.

FRANCIS. Right.

Pause.

CUPID. So did she get my text?

FRANCIS. Yes.

CHARLIE *enters.*

CHARLIE. Alright ladies, you started without me.

CUPID. Couldn't wait forever, Charlie-boy.

CHARLIE (*referring to* FRANCIS). What the fuck's wrong with him?

CUPID. Don't know, Charlie. What's wrong, Francis?

FRANCIS. Nothing.

CHARLIE. You look pretty pissed off.

FRANCIS. No I'm fine.

CHARLIE. You look like you just found out that Cupy's been fucking your bird. Raise ten.

FRANCIS. I think back to Charlie's sister getting raped and it calms me down. I fold.

Scene Twelve

Music is playing loudly in another room.

CUPID drags in LILLY, who is resisting. She is wearing a short skirt. FRANCIS follows.

LILLY. Get off me.

CUPID. Close the door, Francis, and for fuck's sake make sure it's locked this time.

FRANCIS closes and locks the door.

LILLY. So how long has this been going on?

CUPID. There's nothing going on Lilly, you're drunk.

LILLY. You know what, I must be, 'cause from where I was standing it looked like you had Francis's dick in your mouth.

CUPID. You ever say anything like that again, I'll cut your fucking tits off.

LILLY. I'm leaving.

LILLY goes to leave.

CUPID. You're not going anywhere.

CUPID restrains her.

LILLY. You touch me again, I'm telling Charlie everything.

FRANCIS. For fuck's sake Lilly, just shut up. When are you going to learn to shut the fuck up?

LILLY. Don't talk to me, don't ever talk to me. You make me feel sick, sucking each other off.

CUPID. You better shut up, Lilly.

LILLY (*to* CUPID) Suppose I was lucky that I didn't walk in ten minutes later, you'd have been fucking. Have you let him fuck you yet Cupid or did . . .

CUPID *grabs* LILLY *and kisses her, ripping part of her shirt.*

LILLY (*screams*). Charlie!

CUPID *hits* LILLY *across the face and she falls on the floor, semiconscious.*

Pause.

CUPID *looks at* FRANCIS.

CUPID. You staying?

Pause.

Scene Thirteen

CHARLIE. Right, so I'm just about to go to this fancy-dress party and I'm all dressed up like an SS guard when this bird I know calls, asking if I wanted to come round, keep her company. So I wash my cock and go round there but she's having none of it, so I bend her over her kid's Tomy playhouse and do her and she's all like screaming and crying and shit so I pick her up and smash her head against the wall and there's blood everywhere and she's laying on the floor and I'm fucked 'cause this costume's hired and I think all I need now is some anorexic kid watching and I'm living the dream.

CUPID. Okay, there's two of us in this room and this girl is semiconscious on the bed –

FRANCIS. Shut up, Cupid.

CUPID *and* CHARLIE *look at* FRANCIS.

Beat.

CUPID. Don't worry, Francis, it's fine.

FRANCIS. You're not funny.

CUPID. I'm not trying to be funny, Francis, I'm trying to tell my mate a story.

FRANCIS. Don't do it, Cupid.

CHARLIE. Don't do what?

Would someone care to tell me what the fuck's going on?

CUPID. Francis, relax.

FRANCIS. You want to do this now?

Beat.

CUPID. So there's two of us in this room and this girl, this absolute slut is semiconscious on the bed, and because she's pissed, her skirt, which was too fucking short anyway, is like up around her stomach and both of us are thinking the same thing and the air is fucking electric.

Short pause.

So I fuck her hard, 'cause you know, you draw a flush, you've got to take it. And then I turn her over and keep on fucking her until she stops fighting. And when I walk out, I don't even look at her.

Scene Fourteen

FRANCIS *is holding a mobile to his ear.*

FRANCIS. So I leave it ten rings but she doesn't answer.

HOLLY *enters.*

Where have you been?

HOLLY. Where have I been? Where do you think I've been? You didn't meet me.

FRANCIS. I didn't stay. I've been trying to ring you.

HOLLY. I didn't take my phone.

FRANCIS. Well that was stupid, what if you'd broken down?

HOLLY. I didn't.

FRANCIS. But you could have.

HOLLY. But I didn't.

FRANCIS. I know, but you could have.

HOLLY. But I didn't.

FRANCIS. Oh for fuck's sake, I'm sorry for worrying. Jesus.

Pause.

Yeah alright, I'm sorry.

HOLLY. Don't worry about it. Your mum told me about the
anniversary.

FRANCIS. What?

HOLLY. Your friend. It's her anniversary.

FRANCIS. It was yesterday.

HOLLY. How did she die?

Beat.

FRANCIS. Hit by a car, coming back from a party.

HOLLY. What, the car was?

FRANCIS. No, she was.

Beat.

HOLLY. Were you at the party?

FRANCIS. Yeah.

HOLLY. Did you get to say goodbye to her?

FRANCIS. What?

HOLLY. I just wondered if you can remember what the last
thing you said to her was.

Pause.

FRANCIS. Can't remember.

Pause.

HOLLY. Do you want a blowjob?

Beat.

FRANCIS. Okay.

HOLLY *goes down on* FRANCIS.

(*Mournfully.*) She gives me blowjobs all the time. Once, she wouldn't give me this magazine she was reading, so I asked for a blowjob and when she came over, I stole it from her.

FRANCIS *laughs for a few seconds then starts to cry.*

HOLLY. What's wrong?

Beat.

FRANCIS (*still crying*). Nothing.

Beat.

HOLLY. It's okay.

FRANCIS. I know.

Pause.

HOLLY *leaves.* FRANCIS *dries his eyes.*

FRANCIS. So she's lying on my chest in bed, 'cause Holly loves falling asleep on me, and I'm cuddling her and out of nowhere she tells me about her first time. 'Cause she was only sixteen at this party and she was drunk. And this bloke and his mate decide to take advantage. And she tells me about it and I listen to her.

I listen to everything.

And I think about it and I imagine it. And I want to cry.

And after a while she falls asleep.

And I begin to sob my heart and I hold her and kiss her and cry like I've never. Or will ever. And she wakes up and asks me what's the matter. But all I can do is cry.

So I write a confession and address it to Charlie, but that doesn't do it justice. So I go out and I lose a hundred and twenty quid. But that doesn't do it justice. So the next night I go out and lose a hundred and fifty quid, but that doesn't do it justice. So the next night I go out and hit some ex-public-school boy and when he doesn't get up I hit his friend and when he doesn't get up I start on someone else, but that doesn't do it justice and I start to realise what this is I've got to carry around. And I start to realise how fucking long my life is and I walk straight to the top of a multi-storey and I honest to God think about jumping off. But that doesn't do it justice, so I jump.

And when I hit the ground I die.

And I lay back and think thank fuck for that.

And everything is quiet.

Beautifully quiet.

And everyone wishes they'd died sooner.

And I float.

And I kiss my mother and she is crying, and I kiss my dad and my sister and they are crying and they wave me goodbye and I float.

Scene Fifteen

CHARLIE *is reading a piece of paper.*

Silence.

CUPID. Alright Charlie, anything interesting?

CHARLIE. Yeah Cupid, it is. It's a letter from Francis.

Pause.

You got a gun, Cupid?

CUPID. No Charlie, not on me.

Beat.

I could get you one.

CHARLIE. I got to kill someone.

CUPID. Yeah.

Pause.

Then what?

CHARLIE (*slowly and tearfully*). I'll buy a bike, a big shiny
    fucking bike and I'll get the ferry to France and drive down
    across the Bordeaux region 'cause I fucking love wine. And
    I'll play poker, and after a few setbacks I'll work up a
    bankroll of fifty grand except it'll be in euros, and then I'll
    bet it all on one hand and everyone will think I'm mental
    'cause the odds are stacked against me but I'll win and
    they'll be like 'Jesus, that was lucky' and I'll look at them
    as if to say 'I know what the fuck I am doing' and they'll be
    all like 'do you know anything about that guy Skinny Luke?'
    and they'll go 'no, he just turned up on his motorbike and
    cleaned us out.'

Beat.

'Cause I'll change my name to Skinny Luke.

And I'll start a scooter-hire business in Gibraltar and I'll
    build it up from nothing and I'll get a wife and some kids
    and a fucking big pool that's filled with saltwater 'cause
    chlorine makes me cry, and people will look at me like a
    man who's got everything but I just look into the distance
    'cause I know that sooner or later MI6 or Interpol or the
    FBI are going to knock on my door and they'll be all like
    'alright Charlie' and my wife will be all like 'who the fuck's
    Charlie?' and I'll go 'okay boys, you got me' but then when
    I get in the car I'll beat the shit out of them and speed off
    and I'll be crying and shit 'cause I know I'll never see my
    kids again.

Never.

Pause.

I don't have a gun, Cupid.

CUPID. No.

Beat.

CHARLIE. Was it worth it?

CUPID. Are you going to kill me?

CHARLIE. No.

CUPID. I'm a bloke aren't I.

CHARLIE. What's that got to do with anything?

Pause.

It's probably better if we don't see each other from now on.

CUPID. Yeah.

Beat.

CHARLIE. I'll miss you.

CUPID. Yeah.

CHARLIE. We're pretty good mates.

CUPID. Yeah.

Beat.

CHARLIE *exits.*

Beat.

CUPID. So I'm sitting in this bar and I feel like shit all the time and there's this big fat black woman and she starts singing and there's piano and I listen and she's singing like some fucking oracle or something.

'Cause it's playing my heart and all of sudden there's strings and I want to cry . . . and phone my mum . . . and believe in something for once 'cause I've never heard anything like it and this big black gospel just opens up and swallows the whole fucking room and I just want to hold her tongue with both hands and stroke it and watch it work

and rest my face on it and I want to get a job and protect
my family and all that 'cause for that song that's what
I wanted and I could see it. I could fucking smell it and
touch it and feel it in my hands.

And when it ends I look round and nothing happened.

Pause.

And the next day I wake up and nothing . . .

And the day after that . . .

And I continue for a few years . . .

And I walk around but . . .

Beat.

And one day I realise I'm old. And it occurs to me that I'm
walking to the top of a multi-storey.

And the view is unremarkable.

And I get home.

And I sleep.

Lights slowly fade to black.

A Nick Hern Book

Flush first published in Great Britain as a paperback original
in 2004 by Nick Hern Books Limited, 14 Larden Road,
London W3 7ST in association with Soho Theatre, London

Flush copyright © 2004 David Dipper

David Dipper has asserted his right to be identified as
the author of this work

Cover image © VCL/Antonio Mo/Getty Images

Typeset by Country Setting, Kingsdown, Kent CT14 8ES
Printed and bound in Great Britain by Cox and Wyman Limited,
Reading, Berks

A CIP catalogue record for this book is available from
the British Library

ISBN 1 85459 815 5

CAUTION All rights whatsoever in this play are strictly
reserved. Requests to reproduce the text in whole or in part should
be addressed to the publisher.

Amateur Performing Rights Applications for performance,
including readings and excerpts, in the English language throughout
the world by amateurs (excluding stock companies in the United
States of America and Canada) should be addressed to the
Performing Rights Manager, Nick Hern Books, 14 Larden Road,
London W3 7ST, *fax* +44 (0)20 8735 0250,
e-mail info@nickhernbooks.demon.co.uk, except as follows:

Australia: Dominie Drama, 8 Cross Street, Brookvale 2100,
fax (2) 9905 5209, *e-mail* dominie@dominie.com.au

New Zealand: Play Bureau, PO Box 420, New Plymouth,
fax (6) 753 2150, *e-mail* play.bureau.nz@xtra.co.nz

Professional Performing Rights Applications for performance
by professionals in any medium and in any language throughout
the world (including by stock companies in the United States
of America and Canada) should be addressed to The Rod Hall
Agency Limited, 3 Charlotte Mews, London W1T 4DZ,
e-mail office@rodhallagency.com

No performance of any kind may be given unless a licence has
been obtained. Applications should be made before rehearsals
begin. Publication of this play does not necessarily indicate its
availability for performance.